COULD YOU SURVIVE
THE ICE AGE?
AN INTERACTIVE PREHISTORIC ADVENTURE

WRITTEN BY BLAKE HOENA
ILLUSTRATED BY ALESSANDRO VALDRIGHI

Raintree is an imprint of Capstone Global Library Limited, a company incorporated in England and Wales having its registered office at 264 Banbury Road, Oxford, OX2 7DY – Registered company number: 6695582

www.raintree.co.uk
myorders@raintree.co.uk

Edited by Mandy Robbins
Designed by Bobbie Nuytten
Original illustrations © Capstone Global Library Limited 2021
Picture research by Jo Miller
Production by Tori Abraham
Originated by Capstone Global Library Ltd
Printed and bound in India

ISBN: 978 1 4747 9337 7

British Library Cataloguing in Publication Data
A full catalogue record for this book is available from the British Library.

CONTENTS

INTRODUCTION

YOU are an ordinary child going about your everyday life. Suddenly you find yourself in a strange place and a strange time. It's a period from long ago. The world looks different from anything you've ever seen before. Terrifying beasts roam the land. Danger lurks at every turn. Where will you find shelter? How will you get food? Will you ever see your friends and family again? Most importantly of all, can you survive?

Chapter one sets the scene. Then you choose which path to take. Follow the directions at the bottom of each page. The choices you make determine what happens next. When you have finished your path, go back and read the others for more adventures.

YOU CHOOSE the path you take through the Ice Age!

Turn the page to begin your adventure.

CHAPTER 1

THE MUSEUM OF NATURAL HISTORY

You and your classmates are going on a class trip to the Museum of Natural History.

"I can't wait to see the displays," your friend Jayla says.

"I'm just happy to be getting out of our lessons today," Mateo jokes.

You and Jayla roll your eyes.

Mr Andrist stands at the front of the bus.

"Okay, children," he says, "when we get off the bus, a museum guide will lead you through exhibits of the Pleistocene Epoch."

Turn the page.

You have already learned in your lessons that this period of Earth's history started about 2.5 million years ago. It marked the beginning of the last Ice Age and lasted until about 12,000 years ago.

In Mr Andrist's lesson, you have studied animals called megafauna that lived during the Pleistocene Epoch. Many were giant versions of modern-day animals, such as the cave bear and the sabre-toothed cat. This time period is also when modern-day humans evolved.

When Mr Andrist stops talking, your classmates file off the bus. In front of the museum's glass doors stands a young woman with a name tag that reads "Rebecca".

"Hello! I am one of the palaeontologists on staff at the museum," she says. "Does everyone know what a palaeontologist does?"

"You study old things," Mateo says.

The children around you chuckle quietly.

"Well, yes," Rebecca says. "Though, here at the museum, I also get to share my knowledge with budding scientists such as yourselves."

Rebecca shows you displays of Ice Age people and animals. You learn that in Europe, Neanderthals became extinct about 40,000 years ago, shortly after modern-day humans called Cro-Magnons arrived. Camels called camelops roamed western parts of North America. Australia had giant crocodiles and lizards.

After lunch, you line up in a long corridor. You manoeuvre to the front with Jayla and Mateo. There are three doorways with a sign above each one. One sign says "North America", another reads "Europe" and the last reads "Australia".

Turn the page.

"This ends the guided part of your tour," Rebecca says. "But your adventure isn't over yet."

She goes on to explain that you are going to learn about the last glacial period, which began almost 100,000 years ago and ended about 12,000 years ago. During this time in North America, glaciers covered most of Canada and extended south into the United States. Northern parts of Europe and Asia were also covered in these mountain-sized sheets of slow-moving ice. Even Australia was affected by the cold temperatures.

"At the end of this corridor are three doorways," she adds. "Each one holds an exhibit about a different part of the world. Go ahead and explore, but please don't touch the artefacts. They are very old and fragile." Rebecca pauses before adding, "And some are rather special."

Jayla turns to you and Mateo and asks, "Which one shall we go and see first?"

"It doesn't matter to me," Mateo says.

Both friends look to you to decide.

To go to the North American display, turn the page.

To go to the European display, turn to page 45.

To go to the Australian display, turn to page 69.

CHAPTER 2

NORTH AMERICA

You point to the doorway with the sign that says "North America".

"Let's find out how things were in North America," you say.

"Yes, great idea," Jayla says.

Just before reaching the doorway, you see a map of North America on the wall. Jayla leans in to read a plaque below the map.

"It says the last glacial period reached its peak about 20,000 to 25,000 years ago," she says. "During this time, the Laurentide and Cordilleran Ice Sheets covered most of Canada and parts of the United States."

Turn the page.

The doorway opens up into a large exhibit of a scene from prehistoric times. There is a woolly mammoth and a sabre-toothed cat. You and your friends wander over to a diorama of a village of Clovis people. They are believed to be some of the first people to live in North America. In front of the display, you notice something odd on the ground. It looks like a spear dropped from one of the figures in the diorama. The three of you all seem to be drawn to the spear. You know you're not supposed to, but you bend down to pick it up at the same time.

As you touch the spear, you feel a slight tingle in your fingers. Then a cool breeze wraps around you. You shiver.

"Did you feel that?" Jayla asks.

"Brrr," Mateo says. "It feels like we are in the Ice Age."

You look back at your friends and are surprised to see them standing on the edge of a rocky cliff. A river rages beneath it.

"I think we are!" you blurt out in shock. You glance around at your new surroundings and feel a cold gust tousle your hair.

"What happened to the museum?" Mateo cries out in fear.

"I don't know," Jayla answers nervously. "But I know I want to get down from here!"

To your right the ground slopes into flat plains as far as the eye can see. To your left the ground rolls into grassy hills with brush and trees dotted throughout.

To head towards the plains, turn the page.
To walk along the rolling hills, turn to page 19.

"It will probably be easier to walk in the flatlands," you say. "Let's go right."

For a while, it's easy going, if a bit boring. But after an hour or so, the ground behind you begins to rumble.

"What's that?" Mateo asks. "An earthquake?"

"Worse," Jayla answers. "Mammoths!"

You spin around to see a group of woolly mammoths with shaggy fur and incredibly long tusks trotting your way.

"We really are in the Ice Age!" you exclaim.

The lead mammoth raises its head and lets out a deafening sound through its trunk.

"I don't think it likes us," you whisper.

The mammoth trumpets again and takes another step forward.

Turn the page.

"It's going to charge," Jayla says.

"What shall we do?" Mateo asks.

You could turn and run. Running might make a predator think you are prey. But mammoths are plant eaters. You doubt it would chase you. Or would it? Maybe you should stand your ground. Waving your arms and making noise can scare off some animals.

To turn and run, turn to page 22.
To stand your ground, turn to page 23.

"The hills seem safer," you say. "We can hide from predators there. Let's go left."

You walk on for about an hour, when Jayla suddenly gasps. Lurking in the grass in front of you is a large cat with two very long canine teeth. It snarls menacingly.

"Oh no," Mateo whispers as he gulps in fear. "Is that a sabre-toothed cat?"

"It certainly looks like one," Jayla says.

The cat crouches back on its haunches and growls. You know that sabre-toothed cats are carnivores, just like modern-day big cats. They eat other animals for food. You now realize that not only can you hide from predators in the hills, they can hide from you, too.

"What shall we do?" Jayla asks.

Turn the page.

You could make a run for it, hoping that people aren't part of a sabre-toothed cat's diet. Or you can stand your ground, hoping that three children are too threatening for the cat to risk attacking.

To stand your ground, turn to page 27.

To turn and run, turn to page 31.

Woolly mammoths, like modern-day elephants, eat plants, not animals. The mammoth wouldn't think of you as prey, so you turn and run.

"Come on!" you shout to your friends.

All three of you start running. What you didn't realize is that by turning your back on the mammoth, you are showing signs of fear. The mammoth trumpets again, and the beasts lumber after you, hoping to drive you off.

You run as fast as you can, but you are no match for the big beasts. Suddenly you feel a tusk swipe at you. You fly into the air. When you crash back to the ground, the wind has been knocked out of you. You can't get out of the way as the mammoths trample you to death.

THE END

To follow another path, turn to page 11.
To learn more about the Ice Age, turn to page 99.

You know that it is best not to run from predators. But pretending to be intimidating can actually scare them off. Maybe that would work for a woolly mammoth, too.

"Do what I do," you tell your friends. You wave your hands over your head and shout, "No! No! No!" as loud as you can.

"Stop! Stop! Stop!" Jayla shouts as she jumps up and down.

"Don't be a woolly bully," Mateo shouts as he waves his arms back and forth.

The mammoth looks like it is not sure about you or what it should do. Then it trumpets one last time before turning and walking away. The rest of the herd follows. You breathe a sigh of relief as they lumber off in the other direction.

"Phew, that was scary," Jayla says.

Turn the page.

"I can't believe we just faced down a herd of woolly mammoths," Mateo says. "No one will believe this."

"If we don't work out how to get back to the museum, we won't have anyone to tell," you say.

You wonder what to do next. Somehow, you travelled back in time to when woolly mammoths roamed the earth. What other dangers might you run into?

"We should find shelter or water," Jayla says.

Glancing around, you see the sun glinting off what you think might be water in the distance.

"Let's go that way," you say, pointing towards a spot on the horizon. "I think I can see water."

After walking for a time, you reach a wide river. You bend down to scoop up a handful of water to drink.

Turn the page.

When everyone has relieved their thirst, Jayla says, "We still need shelter."

"And to find a way home," Mateo adds.

You know that as long as you stay close to the river, you will have water. But to find shelter, and possibly a way back to your own time, you have no idea what to do or where to head. Should you follow the river north or south?

To go north, turn to page 32.
To go south, turn to page 34.

You could never outrun a sabre-toothed cat. And if you did run, it might think you are prey and pounce. So you decide to stand your ground and hope that the three of you can scare the cat away.

"Do what I do," you say to your friends.

You raise your arms, trying to look as big as you can. Then you shout at the top of your lungs.

"Go away! Shoo! Scram!" Jayla shouts as she jumps up and down.

"You big scaredy-cat!" Mateo shouts as he waves his arms about.

The sabre-toothed cat stops. It looks unsure about what to do. It growls as you continue to shout and scream, but it slowly slinks backwards. You don't stop what you are doing until the cat turns and pads away.

Turn the page.

"Wow, I can't believe that worked," Jayla says.

"No one's going to mess with us now," Mateo says. "Not even a T rex."

"Don't worry about that. Dinosaurs became extinct long before the Ice Age," you say.

Now that the present danger is over, you have to work out what to do next. Somehow, you ended up back during a time when sabre-toothed cats lived. You are sure there are other dangerous prehistoric beasts.

"We should seek shelter or find water," Jayla says, and then she points to something off in the distance. "That looks like a river."

You see sunlight glinting off the waves. "Let's head that way."

"As long as we head in the opposite direction to the sabre-toothed cat, I'm happy," Mateo says.

Turn the page.

You walk for more than an hour before coming to a raging river. There is no way you can swim across. To continue on, you need to follow it to the north or south. Glancing in either direction, all you see is grassland stretching out to the horizon.

"Does it matter which way we go?" Mateo asks.

Jayla looks to the south and then to the north.

"I can't see much of a difference," she adds. "But as long as we stay close to the river, we'll have water.

To turn north, turn to page 32.
To turn south, turn to page 34.

You don't want to stick around to find out if Ice Age cat food includes humans. It's best to run.

"Let's make a run for it," you whisper.

Jayla and Mateo both nod. The cat snarls again and paws at the ground.

"Go!" you shout.

You, Mateo and Jayla make a break for it. What you didn't realize is that by running, the sabre-toothed cat thinks you're prey. You don't get very far before you feel it slam you to the ground. Then two sharp, knife-like teeth dig into your neck and shoulder. The sabre-toothed cat quickly ends your life.

THE END

To follow another path, turn to page 11.
To learn more about the Ice Age, turn to page 99.

You don't know where you are, so one direction seems as good as another.

"Then let's go this way," you say, turning north. You follow the river as it winds north.

Walking along, you rarely see any other animals, and you don't see any other people. As the days pass, your feet and legs get sore. The grumbling of your stomach reminds you how hungry you are. But in the end, it is not prehistoric beasts or hunger that leads to your downfall. The further you travel north, the colder the temperatures get.

Then one day, you see a mountainous cliff of ice blocking your path. It is then that you realize the river you had been following was created by glacier water.

"That glacier must be extremely thick," Jayla says.

"I can't go any further," Mateo says, dropping to his knees.

"It was a mistake to come this way," you mumble to yourself.

You realize you should have been travelling south, away from the glaciers. You rest under the shadow of the looming mountain of ice. That night, a storm rolls in. The area is blanketed in snow. You and your friends huddle together for warmth. But it's no good. Everyone is shivering violently. Hypothermia sets in as your body temperature drops. Slowly, each of you drifts off to sleep, never to wake again.

THE END

To follow another path, turn to page 11.
To learn more about the Ice Age, turn to page 99.

"Let's go south," you say. "If this is the Ice Age, we don't want to head north. That's where the glaciers are."

"Makes sense to me," Mateo says.

Your group turns south, following the river. You have water to drink whenever you are thirsty. But you are unsure about eating any of the berries or plants you see. They could be poisonous. Soon your stomachs are grumbling.

"Let's take a break," Mateo says after a while. "I'm so tired."

You have no idea where you are or where you are going. What's the harm in stopping?

"Okay," you say.

All three of you are tired, sweaty and hungry. You flop to the ground.

"Ouch," Mateo shouts, swatting at an insect. "These prehistoric mosquitoes are huge!"

"Quiet, I think I hear something," Jayla says.

The three of you listen quietly. Over the sound of the water and the buzz of insects, you think you hear voices.

"It's people," Mateo says.

"We should go and investigate," Jayla says.

You walk quietly in the direction of the voices. You keep your heads down and duck behind bushes as you creep along. Then you crawl up a hill and peek over the top of it.

In the distance you see a large fire in the middle of a small village. The shelters look a bit like Native American tepees, but they seem to be built out of plant materials.

Turn the page.

"They might be Neanderthals," Mateo says.

"No, they lived in Europe, not North America," Jayla says.

"They are the Clovis," you say. "Like the people in the diorama back at the museum."

You don't know much about these ancient people. You certainly won't understand their language, and you don't know if they're friendly. Maybe it would be safest to avoid them. But then, you don't have any food, shelter or any way to start a fire. The people in the village have everything you need.

To avoid the village, turn the page.
To go and meet the Clovis, turn to page 40.

You barely survived an encounter with a dangerous prehistoric animal. You don't think it's worth the risk of meeting prehistoric people. They may not be any friendlier than the beast you faced.

"It looks like they have food," Mateo says hopefully.

"But look, they also have weapons," you say, pointing to their spears.

Mateo and Jayla nod in agreement. The three of you sneak back down the hill and quietly make your way along the river. You are careful not to be seen or heard by the people of the village.

While you are able to avoid other people and large animals, you are constantly struggling to feed yourself. You spend almost all of your time looking for food.

The days turn into weeks and the weeks into months. Slowly you give up on ever returning back to the museum or seeing your classmates and family again. You and your friends spend the rest of your lives just trying to survive the harsh environment of the Ice Age.

THE END

To follow another path, turn to page 11.
To learn more about the Ice Age, turn to page 99.

"I think we should go to the village," you say. "The people there can't be worse than facing a sabre-toothed cat or a woolly mammoth."

"And I'm hungry," Mateo says.

"Plus they have a fire," Jayla adds.

"I don't think we have any other choice," you say.

The three of you begin walking towards the village. Soon you hear shouting. Several men armed with spears come running towards you. They shout at you in a language you don't understand. You and your friends do your best to keep calm.

You raise your hands in front of you and quietly say, "We mean you no harm."

"We are cold," Jayla says, pointing to the fire.

"And hungry," Mateo says, motioning with one hand towards his open mouth.

Turn the page.

After a few tense moments, the prehistoric people stop shouting and shaking their spears at you. One man waves you forward towards the fire, where you take a seat. A little while later, a woman brings each of you a bowl of food. She motions by bringing her hand to her mouth.

"She wants us to eat," Jayla says.

"What is it?" Mateo asks, looking at his bowl.

You are too hungry to care. It's food and you're starving. As you eat, one of the men squats down next to you. He sets his spear on the ground between you and your friends. You all look at it and then at each other with a shock of familiarity. It certainly looks like the spear you touched at the museum. At the same time, all three of you reach over and touch it. Suddenly you feel a familiar tingle. The air shimmers around you.

In an instant, the crackle of the fire is replaced by the excited voices of your friends.

"We're back!" Mateo exclaims.

You find yourself in the museum standing next to the fallen spear. Just then, Rebecca walks past. She takes a pair of gloves out of her pocket and puts them on. Then she bends down to pick up the spear.

"This is one of those special artefacts," she says, with a wink. "I'd better put it somewhere safe."

THE END

To follow another path, turn to page 11.
To learn more about the Ice Age, turn to page 99.

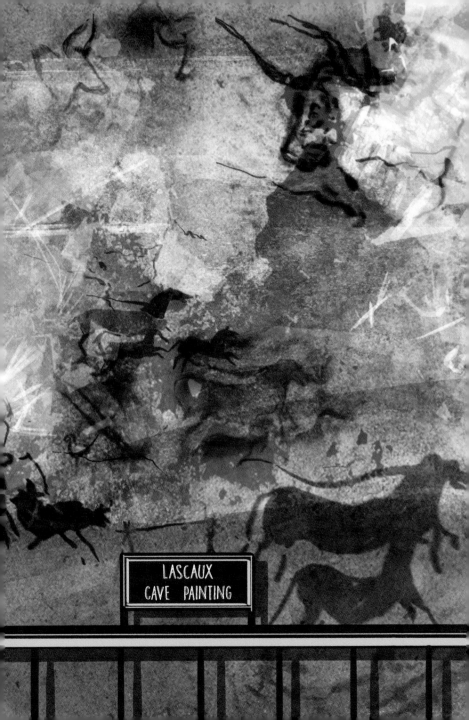

LASCAUX
CAVE PAINTING

CHAPTER 3

EUROPE

"Let's go to Europe," you say. "I want to see what Neanderthals and Cro-Magnon people looked like."

You head towards the Europe display and your friends follow. As you enter the room, Mateo points to something painted on one wall.

"What are those?" he asks.

"They look like a painting of some sort of animals," you say.

"They're cave paintings," Jayla says. "Like those found in the Lascaux Caves in France."

You walk over to the cave paintings with your friends. You are surprised at how lifelike it looks. The wall appears to be real rock.

Turn the page.

Mesmerized, you and your friends forget about Rebecca's warning and lean in to touch it. You feel a tingle in your fingers. Suddenly you are surrounded by darkness.

"What's happening?" Mateo asks. "Are we still in the museum?"

"I don't know," you say, glancing around. "I don't think so."

"It looks like we're in an actual cave!" Jayla exclaims.

"OK, this is strange," Mateo says.

The only light comes from the sun shining through an entrance on the far side of the cave. As your eyes adjust to the dim light, you see paintings on the walls. They are red and black.

"They look real," Jayla says, inspecting them.

On the ground there are bowls filled with what looks like red and black paste. In the middle of the cave are the remains of a fire.

"Let's see what's outside," Mateo says, stepping through the entrance. "This cave is really creepy."

You and Jayla follow him. Outside is a tundra-like landscape of shrubs and grasses. You can't see any glaciers in the mountainous ridges around you, but you feel the bite of cold air.

"Brr," Jayla says. "It feels as though we're in the Ice Age."

You have an odd feeling that she might be right. There is a village a bit further down in the valley. A group of people have gathered below you. They are covered in furs and some carry spears with stone tips. They look shorter and a little bit more stout than modern-day humans.

Turn the page.

"They might be Cro-Magnons," Jayla explains.

Suddenly Mateo screams. He has stumbled and is tumbling down into the valley.

"Mateo!" you shout.

You and Jayla quickly scramble down after him in a panic. By the time you get to the bottom of the valley, Mateo is surrounded by the strangers. The surprised people are helping him to his feet.

"Are you hurt?" you ask.

"Just a little bruised," Mateo says. "Thankfully these people seem friendly."

"Maybe they will take us in," Jayla says. "It's probably strange to see three children wandering alone – especially in these clothes."

A man and a woman approach you. The man offers you a spear while the woman holds out some wooden bowls.

"I think they want us to either go on a hunt or help them find food," you say.

To go on a hunt, turn the page.
To help gather food, turn to page 52.

"It would be exciting to go on a hunt," you say. "Perhaps we'll see some prehistoric animals."

You and your friends each grab a spear. The man leads you and a group of hunters to a watering hole. You hide in the brush and wait. Eventually you hear a distant trumpeting sound. You peek through the leaves to see several woolly mammoths heading towards you. The ground shakes.

Everyone stays hidden until the beasts get close to the watering hole. Then one man lunges forward from his hiding spot and stabs the nearest mammoth. It trumpets angrily and rises up on its hind legs.

The mammoth is vulnerable. It seems like a good time to join in the attack. Or should you wait to see what the other hunters do?

To wait, turn to page 54.
To hunt, turn to page 58.

"I don't know how to use a spear," you say.

"And I'd rather not run into any wild animals," Jayla adds.

Mateo nods in agreement.

You each grab one of the bowls and follow the woman. Some Cro-Magnon children and other women join you.

While everyone else wanders off searching for berries and other edible plants, the woman guides you over to some shrubs. She shows you which berries to pick and which to leave alone.

Time passes, and you are lost in thought as you pick berries off the bushes. You glance up when you hear a loud huff near you. Staring at you from across a small clearing is the biggest hairy face you have ever seen.

"Jayla," you whisper. "What is that?"

"A cave bear," she says, already frozen in fear.

The bear steps forward, crushing the shrubs in front of it. It's huge! On all fours, it stands as tall as you. It is stocky, and you guess it weighs as much as a small car.

"What do they eat?" you ask.

"I think they're omnivores," Jayla replies.

While there are plenty of plants around, you and your friends are the only "meat" nearby.

"I hope it's in the mood for a salad," Mateo says.

You need to get away from the bear. You could throw your bowl of fruit down and make a run for it. Hopefully the bear would be more interested in the berries than in you. Or you could put the bowl down and back away slowly.

To throw the berries and run, turn to page 59.
To slowly back away, turn to page 60.

You look at the other hunters. Even though the mammoth has its tummy exposed, they don't move in for the kill. They seem to be waiting for something. You should probably follow their lead.

The injured mammoth trumpets angrily again. It drops on all fours and then spins around. The herd flees the waterhole.

You and the other hunters follow in pursuit. Every now and then the herd stops. This gives the hunters a chance to attack the injured animal. They launch spears at it from a safe distance. However, the men seem content to simply follow the herd.

"I think they're hoping to wear it out," Jayla says.

She's right. It takes hours, but eventually the mammoth tires from the constant harassment of the hunters. It is slowed by its injuries and struggles to defend itself. That is when the hunters go in for the kill.

When the hunt is complete, other members of the tribe join you. They help to butcher the beast and prepare the meat and its hide. These tasks take the rest of the day.

By nightfall, you are back in the cave. A fire is lit, and you and your friends huddle around it for warmth.

You look at the wall with the cave paintings.

"Maybe we should paint a scene from the hunt today," you say.

Turn the page.

"There's paint," Jayla says, pointing to the bowls along the wall.

Mateo jumps up and heads over to the wall.

"There are brushes, too," he says, holding up some sticks with hair attached to one end.

You walk over to your friend and grab one of the brushes and the bowl of red paint.

"What are you going to paint?" Jayla asks.

"One of the mammoths," you say.

You dip the brush into the paint. When you touch the wall with it, you feel a familiar tingle in your fingers.

Suddenly it is a lot brighter and noisier. The sounds of your excited classmates surround you. Jayla and Mateo are next to you.

Turn to page 67.

With the mammoth exposing its underside, you see an opportunity to attack and impress the other hunters. You stand up from your hiding spot and lunge forward with your spear. As you do, the mammoth drops back to all fours. While the mammoth may be injured, the huge beast is far from defeated. It takes a swipe at you with its long tusks. You are lifted into the air and thrown to the ground.

As you struggle to get to your feet, the herd turns to flee. You are caught in their path. Stampeding feet crash all around you. One lands on your leg. Bones shatter under the mammoth's weight. Then another foot lands on your chest, crushing the life out of you.

THE END

To follow another path, turn to page 11.
To learn more about the Ice Age, turn to page 99.

As the bear takes a step closer, you instinctively step backwards.

"Let's run for it," you tell your friends. "I am going to throw my berries at it, and then let's go."

Out of the corner of your eyes, you see Jayla and Mateo nod.

"Here goes nothing," you say, pulling your arm back. When you throw the bowl, you shout, "Go!"

As you turn your back, the beast gives chase. You run as fast as you can. But you are no match for the speedy bear. It catches your heel in its mouth. You stumble to the ground, and the bear is upon you. It strikes with bone-crushing blows. One paw catches you across the head, and the blow knocks you out. You fall to the ground, never to wake again.

THE END

To follow another path, turn to page 11.
To learn more about the Ice Age, turn to page 99.

You worry what the bear might do if you make any sudden moves. It might attack if you startle it. So you try to remain calm.

"Slowly put down your bowls," you tell your friends.

Out of the corner of your eyes, you see Jayla and Mateo do as you say. The bear huffs as it sniffs the air. It can probably smell what's in the bowls.

"Now calmly back away," you instruct your friends.

Each one of you takes a step back. The cave bear just watches. You take another step, and still the bear does nothing.

"How are you feeling?" you ask your friends.

"I'm about to wet myself," Mateo says, taking another step.

Turn the page.

"Can we run yet?" Jayla asks, stepping back.

"No, not yet," you say. "Just keep walking backwards."

As you continue to back away, the bear moves in to sniff the bowls. It's distracted, but you're not safe yet. The three of you keep backing away slowly until the bear is out of sight.

You go to find the woman who brought you here. You do your best to tell her about the bear while Mateo stands behind you growling and raising his hands in the air. The woman looks from you to him, and you think she understands. She says something urgent to the other people. They quickly gather up everything that they had collected, and the woman leads everyone back to the village.

When you're back, Jayla points to the cave.

"We should make a cave painting of our adventure," she says.

"But the villagers are preparing a meal with the food they have gathered," Mateo replies. "We should have something to eat first."

While you think it would be fun to do a cave painting, you are also feeling hungry.

To eat with the villagers, turn the page.
To go back to the cave, turn to page 66.

You can't remember the last time you ate. And even though all the villagers have is some berries and seeds, that is better than being hungry.

The woman you met earlier motions you to sit down next to the fire. Then you are each handed a bowl of food.

As you eat with your fingers, Mateo asks, "Do you think we'll ever get home?"

"I hope so," you say between mouthfuls.

"At least we have everything we need to survive with these people," Jayla says.

You spend the night with the villagers, and in the morning you help them gather food again. While you continue to wonder if you will ever return home, your focus slowly turns to doing what you need to do in order to survive.

Eventually you learn the Cro-Magnon people's ways of life and even their language. You become an adult and marry. You have a few children and sometimes wonder if your memories of the future were all just a dream. You live to old age, spending the rest of your life with the Cro-Magnon people.

THE END

To follow another path, turn to page 11.
To learn more about the Ice Age, turn to page 99.

Just then, you feel a sudden shiver. The sun is setting, and the cold is creeping in. It is a reminder that you are still back in the Ice Age.

"Let's go to the cave for shelter," you say. "And it would be fun to make a cave painting."

Once in the cave, Jayla rushes over to the bowls of red and black paste on the floor. There are also brushes made of some sort of hair.

"Let's paint the cave bear," she says, as she begins her painting. You walk over and grab a bowl of paint and a brush. When you touch the wall with the brush, you feel a familiar tingle shoot up your arm.

Suddenly the air is filled with the sounds of your excited classmates, and bright lights make you squint. You spin around to see that you are back in the museum.

"We're back!" you shout.

You, Jayla and Mateo are standing in front of the museum's cave painting display.

"Did we paint that?" Mateo asks, nodding to the images in front of you.

"I don't know," you say, looking down at the brush in your hand.

Just then, Rebecca walks up to you and grabs the bowl and brush from you.

"Be careful with those," she says. "They are very special artefacts."

THE END

To follow another path, turn to page 11.
To learn more about the Ice Age, turn to page 99.

CHAPTER 4

AUSTRALIA

"Let's go and see the exhibit on Australia," you tell your friends.

"Good idea," replies Mateo. "It's 'the land down under'!"

You have always been interested in Australia. It has some of the world's most amazing animals, from cuddly-looking koalas to monstrous saltwater crocodiles. You can only imagine what type of amazing creatures lived there in prehistoric times.

"Isn't Australia mainly desert?" Mateo asks as he follows you. "I bet it didn't get very cold."

"I bet it did," Jayla says. "It was the Ice Age. I'm sure we'll see some cool animals on display."

Turn the page.

"Like that one!" you say, pointing towards an animal that looks like a giant kangaroo with a short, stubby snout.

"What about that one?" Mateo says, pointing to another exhibit that appears to be part giant wombat and part hairy hippopotamus.

Then you notice a display of ancient tools off to one side.

"Hey, let's look over here," you say to your friends.

You walk over to a glass display case. It is filled with spear tips and axe heads. Most of them look as though they're made out of stone. Then you notice something odd. A knife that looks like it's made out of glass sits on top of the case.

"What's that doing here?" you ask as your friends lean in to see.

You reach over to touch the tool.

"Don't touch anything!" Jayla calls.

Both she and Mateo reach out to stop you from grabbing the knife. They touch you just as you pick up the mesmerizing object. Suddenly you feel a tingle in your finger. Then a wave of energy washes over you.

One moment you are standing in the museum, surrounded by your classmates. The next, you feel the crunch of dry earth under your feet. Glancing around, you are surprised to be in the middle of an enormous desert with mountains lining the distant horizon.

"Oh no, what's happened?" you ask. "It looks as though we're actually in Australia."

"I think we are," Jayla responds. "And I think it's the Ice Age!"

Turn the page.

"No way!" Mateo cries. "How do we get back to the museum?"

"We should probably try and work that out," you say.

You and your friends are in a desert, which seems like the best place to be during an ice age. Deserts are warm, you think. But will you be safe here in a wide-open area? Who knows what sort of prehistoric creatures might be roaming about. There is a mountain range off in the distance. You might find shelter there.

To explore the desert, go to the next page.
To head for the mountains, turn to page 77.

"Let's stick around here," you tell your friends. "We appeared in the desert, so maybe if we stay put, we'll reappear back at the museum."

To pass the time, you and your friends look around for water and food. But you don't have much luck. It is the desert, after all.

Suddenly Mateo shouts, "Hey look!"

You and Jayla spin around to see Mateo pointing at some animals off in the distance. They look like kangaroos, but they are huge. The animals are taller than you. They're stocky and have stubby snouts. They don't hop like you would expect a kangaroo to, but they hobble forwards on their hind feet.

"I think those are Procoptodon," Jayla says. "There was one on display in the museum."

"Do you think they're hungry?" Mateo asks.

Turn the page.

"Don't worry," you say. "Kangaroos are herbivores."

"Even giant ones?" Mateo asks.

"More like prehistoric ones," Jayla says.

You and your friends watch the Procoptodon herd lumber along. Luckily they don't seem to notice you. You are amazed to see such animals in real life.

"We really are in Australia during the Ice Age," you mumble in awe.

"Well, it's a good thing we're in a desert," Mateo says. "At least we won't freeze here."

"That's not necessarily true," Jayla says. "Not all deserts are hot. What about the Gobi Desert in Asia? It can get freezing cold there at night."

Turn the page.

What Jayla says makes you think that you may not have made the right decision to stay in the desert. When the sun sets, it could get very cold. And you already know that there isn't any food or water around. Maybe following the Procoptodon would lead you to a water source. But you also remember one of the most important rules if you are lost – stay put! That makes it easier for someone to find you. But who will find you in this situation? A part of you still hopes that by staying here you will somehow end up back in the museum.

To stay put and wait to be found, turn to page 81.

To head in the direction of the Procoptodon herd, turn to page 83.

You don't want to be out in the open when night falls. You won't have any protection from whatever predators might come out then. And you're pretty sure the temperatures will plummet when the sun sets. This is the Ice Age after all, and the only thing keeping you warm right now is the sun.

"Let's head for those mountains," you say. "Maybe we can find shelter there."

You begin the trek across the desert.

As you are walking, Jayla says, "Did you know that Antarctica is actually a desert?"

"Really? No!" Mateo says. "I thought deserts were hot."

"It's not about how hot an area gets," Jayla explains. "It's how little moisture it gets."

Turn the page.

"It took thousands of years for Antarctica to get covered in all that ice and snow," you add.

As you reach the foothills surrounding the mountains, you start walking through a lightly forested area. When you reach a hilltop, you hear an odd noise.

"Look!" Jayla says, pointing downhill.

There you see a couple of large birds. They easily stand taller than you, and they're stocky enough to weigh more than any of you.

"They look like huge emus," you say.

"I think they're Genyornis," Jayla says. "They're a type of prehistoric flightless bird. There was a fake one on display at the museum."

Just then, you hear Mateo's stomach grumble again.

Turn the page.

"Quiet," you say. "They might hear us."

"I can't help it! I'm hungry," Mateo says.

"I think they're herbivores," Jayla says of the birds. "So we shouldn't be in danger."

That gives you an idea. Maybe if you watch these birds eat you can work out what plants are safe for you. At this point, you would eat almost anything.

But the sun is beginning to set. You can feel it getting colder already. Maybe you should keep your focus on finding shelter instead of food.

To focus on finding shelter, turn to page 86.
To look for food, turn to page 90.

"Don't you two remember what we learned in our survival lesson about getting lost?" you ask your friends.

"Yes, you're supposed to stay put," Jayla says. "Or you might get even more lost."

"Don't forget the rule of three," Mateo adds. "We can survive three days without water and three weeks without food."

"So we should be fine for a little while," Jayla says.

It is settled. You are going to stay where you are in the hope of being found. Maybe Mr Andrist or Rebecca will realize what's happened to you and somehow bring you home.

In the meantime, you do your best to stay calm and comfortable. You see some dried grass and twigs. You wish you knew how to start a fire.

Turn the page.

When the sun sets, the temperature plummets. It's not just cold, it's freezing. You and your friends huddle together for warmth. Your teeth chatter.

You hadn't expected it to get this cold. That's when you remember the other part of the rule of three – you can only survive three hours in extreme weather. And that's about how long you and your friends last before you are overcome by the cold.

THE END

To follow another path, turn to page 11.
To learn more about the Ice Age, turn to page 99.

You're pretty sure no one is going to time travel into the past to find you. And the desert could get freezing cold when the sun goes down. It's best if you find some shelter before evening.

"Let's follow the Procoptodon," you tell your friends. "Maybe they'll lead us to water or somewhere we can find shelter."

Mateo and Jayla nod in agreement. You are able to keep up with the large animals for a while. But as the desert terrain turns to grasslands, you struggle to keep up with them. You lose sight of the giant kangaroos, but Mateo spots other prehistoric animals.

"Hey look!" he shouts. "It's some of those hairy hippo-like animals."

"Yes, Diprotodon," Jayla adds. "We saw one at the museum."

Turn the page.

"They don't look like meat eaters," you say, as you watch them munching on the brush.

Still, you keep your distance. After all, the Diprotodon are about the size of hippos. You don't want to make them angry. As you are walking around the herd, you hear them squeal and grunt excitedly. Then they all start running in your direction.

"There must be a predator coming," Jayla says.

"If it's prehistoric size, we should get out of here!" Mateo says.

You agree with Mateo, but which direction should you run? Do you run away from the danger with the Diprotodon? Or would it be better to get out of their way and head in another direction?

To flee with the Diprotodon, turn to page 92.
To flee in a different direction, turn to page 93.

You remember reading in a survival book the rule of three. People can survive three hours in extreme weather, three days without water and three weeks without food. So while you are hungry, you know that food is not your biggest priority. As the sun begins to dip towards the horizon, you feel the chill in the air. Overnight, it will get freezing cold. You need to find shelter.

"Let's leave the birds alone," you say to your friends. "We need to find shelter."

"Yeah, I'm feeling chilly," Jayla says.

You continue on. The foothills soon turn into mountains. You are partially protected from the wind by the trees. You even think that perhaps you could collect some fallen branches to build a shelter. But then Mateo sees something surprising.

"Look," Mateo says, pointing towards a cave in the side of the mountain.

Out of the dark cave, you see the soft glow of a fire flickering inside. For a moment you worry about who might be in the cave. But the night's chill quickly dispels any fear.

"There are people in there," Jayla whispers.

"Let's hope they are friendly," you say as you lead your friends into the cave.

There you find a group of people sitting around a fire and eating. While they seem suspicious of you, they must see that you are cold. They wave you over to join them by the fire.

As you sit down, you notice a familiar-looking knife lying next to the fire. You and your friends exchange knowing glances.

"It's the knife from the museum!" Mateo says.

Turn the page.

"Is that what sent us back in time?" Jayla asks.

"There's only one way to find out," you say.

You all reach for the knife at the same time. Suddenly the crackling of the fire is replaced by the sounds of your classmates. Instead of sitting in a cave, you find yourself back in the museum.

"We're back!" Jayla says.

Just then, you all realize that you're still clutching the knife. Instantly, you drop it. The noise attracts Rebecca's attention. She walks over and picks up the knife in her gloved hands.

"How did this get here?" she asks. Then she looks at you with a knowing smile. "I'm glad to see it's still here – and that you are, too."

THE END

To follow another path, turn to page 11.
To learn more about the Ice Age, turn to page 99.

"I have an idea," you tell your friends. "What if we follow the birds and eat whatever they eat?"

"I'd prefer a hot dog," Mateo jokes. "But that's probably not an option."

"It's worth a try," Jayla says.

The three of you sit quietly and watch the birds. They tear up plants with their powerful beaks. From where you are, you can't tell what plants exactly they're eating. But after a while, they wander away.

You're about to give up your search for food when you come across a nest hidden in the grass. There is one huge egg in it. You remember seeing an ostrich egg once. This is much bigger than that. And while you are not a fan of raw egg, it will be enough to feed all three of you.

You creep towards the nest. That's when you hear a loud, threatening squawk. You look around to see one of the birds. It must have stayed behind to protect the nest. The bird races towards you before you have a chance to flee. It kicks you hard in the chest. You hear the snap of ribs as you fly through the air. You lose consciousness from the pain, and the bird continues its attack. You never wake again.

THE END

To follow another path, turn to page 11.
To learn more about the Ice Age, turn to page 99.

"If they're running this way to get away from something," you say, "then we should, too."

You and your friends start running, but the Diprotodon quickly overtake you. Mateo shouts as he is knocked to the ground by one of the beasts. You stop to help him to his feet. As you pull him up, the grass parts in front of you. You come face to face with what looks like a giant crocodile.

It must be longer than a minibus! you think.

It sprints forward on its long legs. You are not quick enough to escape its crushing jaws.

The Diprotodon herd was fleeing from a Quinkana, a prehistoric crocodile that hunted on land. You have just become its next meal.

THE END

To follow another path, turn to page 11.
To learn more about the Ice Age, turn to page 99.

You're pretty sure the Diprotodon can run faster than you. You don't want to get trampled by them.

"Let's get out of their way!" you shout to your friends.

You dart to the side of the stampeding herd as the large Diprotodon race past. The speed of the large creatures astonishes you. But they're not the only speedy animals. Right behind them, you see a large, scaly body on long legs. It has a long snout and a large mouth full of sharp teeth.

"Get down before it sees us," you call to your friends.

You all duck down out of sight in the tall grass just in time.

"That lizard must have been as long as a lorry," Mateo says.

Turn the page.

"It wasn't a lizard," Jayla says. "It was a Quinkana – a crocodile that hunted on land."

"What if there are more? Let's get out of here," you say.

You run in the opposite direction, away from the Quinkana. At one point, you come across a small stream. You follow it and are surprised to come upon a small village of people.

"They must be early native people," Jayla says.

You watch them from a safe distance. They have shelters, food and fire – everything that you need to survive.

"Should we approach them?" Jayla asks.

"It's worth the risk if we want to survive," you say. "What other options do we have – to keep wandering around out here and die of starvation or a horrible animal attack?"

Turn the page.

You lead your friends into the village.
The people watch suspiciously as you walk over
to a fire and sit down next to it. A woman and
a man walk over to you. The man looks angry,
but the woman puts her arm in front of him as
if to calm him down. The woman makes hand
gestures to her mouth.

"She wants to know if we're hungry," you say.

"Oh yes!" Mateo says.

You notice then that the man is holding a
familiar-looking knife. Satisfied that you mean
the people no harm, he puts it down nearby.
You and your friends make eye contact.

"Should we touch it?" Jayla asks.

"Maybe the knife is the key to getting back to
the museum," Mateo adds.

"It couldn't hurt to try," you say.

The three of you reach out quickly and touch the knife. As you do, you feel a tingle in your fingers, and then a wave of energy washes over you. Suddenly the sounds of the crackling fire are replaced by that of your excited classmates. Instead of sitting next to a fire, you find yourself standing next to the glass case.

"We're back," Mateo says.

Just then, Rebecca walks up to you and your friends. With gloved hands, she picks up the tool sitting on top of the case.

"I've been looking for that," she says. "This quartz knife is one of those special artefacts I was talking about."

Rebecca winks at you as she walks away.

THE END

To follow another path, turn to page 11.
To learn more about the Ice Age, turn over the page.

CHAPTER 5

THE ICE AGES

Earth's climate naturally goes through cycles of warm and cool periods. Scientists are not exactly sure why. It could be caused by changes in Earth's movement around the sun or changes in the sun itself. Large meteorite impacts, volcanic activity and animal activity are other possible causes. There have been times in Earth's past when it has been so warm that the polar ice caps melted. There have also been times when it has been so cold that much of the planet was covered in ice and snow.

An extended period in which temperatures drop is known as an ice age. During ice ages, snow might not melt because summers are cooler and glaciers expand to cover large areas of land.

There have been several major ice ages throughout Earth's history. The first was the Huronian Ice Age, which happened more than 2 billion years ago. Next was the Cryogenian Ice Age. It began about 850 million years ago. The Andean-Saharan Ice Age was about 450 million years ago and the Karoo Ice Age about 360 million years ago.

Earth is actually in the middle of a fifth major ice age, which began about 2.5 million years ago. It is called the Quaternary Ice Age. It is known for having had several cooling periods during which glaciers expanded, and then warming periods, in which they retreated. These periods last for tens of thousands of years. The last glacial period began about 100,000 years ago and ended about 12,000 years ago. Currently, our planet is in the midst of an interglacial, or warm, period.

During the last glacial period, average temperatures plummeted by about 10 degrees Celsius. With this extreme cooling, glaciers expanded to cover large areas of Antarctica, North and South America, Europe and Asia.

But ice ages affect the planet in ways other than just covering areas in glaciers. As glaciers creep forward, their sheer size and weight reshapes the surface of the planet. They can carve out valleys and lakes and scrape hills from the landscape. Then when glaciers melt, they fill lakes with water, and the soil and rock they pushed up gets left behind in hills.

Ice ages affect plants and animals, too. The Andean-Saharan Ice Age caused Earth's first mass extinction. As the planet cooled over millions of years, about 86 per cent of all plant and animal life died out.

Another mass extinction happened during the Karoo Ice Age. Nearly 75 per cent of plant and animal species died out.

During the last glacial period of the Quaternary Ice Age many large animals such as the woolly mammoth, cave bear and sabre-toothed cat died out. But smaller animals that could more easily adapt to the colder climate were able to survive. Birds migrated to warmer locations.

Humans also adapted to the changing climate. They relocated to escape the bitter cold. They built shelters and used fire to keep warm. Humans also made tools to help them hunt when food was scarce. Since the last glacial period, humans have become the most dominant species on the planet.

While Earth's climate has gone through warm and cool periods, these changes are different from climate change. The planet's natural cycles of cooling and warming occur slowly, over thousands to millions of years. But in just the last 100 years, the average global temperature has risen 0.7 degrees Celsius, largely due to human activity and pollution. This dramatic increase has affected Earth's natural changes.

During the Quaternary Ice Age, scientists estimate that cycles of glacial and interglacial periods are occurring every 100,000 years. There is a cool period lasting about 90,000 years followed by a warm period of about 10,000 years. Under natural circumstances, temperatures should be getting cooler now, leading to a new glacial period. But that's not what is happening.

Human activity is leading to a change in our naturally occurring climate. It could push the next glacial period away for another 100,000 years. This huge change could threaten the world as we know it. Scientists continue to study the effects of climate change and how we might be able to slow or stop it.

TIMELINE OF EARTH'S ICE AGES

4.6 billion years ago •••

4.6 billion years ago ••••• 542 million years ago
PRECAMBRIAN ERA
Life on Earth begins.

542 million years ago •••• 251 million years ago
PALAEOZOIC ERA
*Plants, fish, amphibians and
reptiles begin to populate Earth.*

**2.4 TO 2.1
BILLION YEARS
AGO** During the
Huronian Ice Age;
only single-celled
organisms exist.

**450 TO 420 MILLION
YEARS AGO**
The Andean-Saharan
Ice Age leads to a major
extinction of plants and
animals. More than half
of life on Earth dies out.

**850 TO 630 MILLION
YEARS AGO**
The Cryogenian Ice Age
occurs, probably due to
new, multi-celled life
forms using up much
of the carbon dioxide in
Earth's atmosphere.

**360 TO 260 MILLION
YEARS AGO**
The Karoo Ice Age leads to
another mass extinction
that seems to affect only
sea creatures.

251 million years ago ••• 65 million years ago
MESOZOIC ERA
Dinosaurs dominate Earth.

65 million years ago •••••• present
CENEZOIC ERA
Mammals become the dominant animal life on Earth.

2.5 MILLION YEARS AGO TO PRESENT
The Pleistocene Epoch marks the beginning of the most recent ice age. During this time there are several glacial and interglacial periods.

251 TO 65 MILLION YEARS AGO
Dinosaurs dominate during this time, but it is also the age when mammals, birds and flowering plants develop.

12,000 YEARS AGO TO PRESENT
The Holocene Epoch takes place. Humans become the dominant species on Earth.

OTHER PATHS TO EXPLORE

>>> In the story paths in this book, you and your friends, Jayla and Mateo, travel back into the past. You have adventures during the Ice Age and see different prehistoric animals. But what if, instead of you going back in time, some real megafauna suddenly appeared in the very museum that you are visiting. What would happen then?

>>> Imagine you could travel back to the Ice Age as in the story paths of this book. But instead of suddenly being transported back in time, you can plan ahead. You can bring food, water and any other supplies that you might need. What would you take with you and how might that help your chances of survival?

>>> During the story paths in this book, you spend most of your time with your friends Jayla and Mateo. But what if you were transported back in time into a village of prehistoric people all by yourself? How might you communicate with them, and how might living with people help you survive?

FIND OUT MORE

BOOKS

A Brief Illustrated History of Life on Earth (A Brief Illustrated History), Steve Parker (Raintree, 2018)

Our Hairy Past: Evolution and Life on Earth, Nancy Dickmann (Raintree, 2019)

Science Vs Animal Extinction (Science Fights Back), Nick Hunter (Raintree, 2017)

WEBSITES

www.bbc.co.uk/bitesize/clips/zstc87h
Find out how climate scientists try to predict how future ice ages will develop and affect the landscape.

www.brainpop.com/science/earthsystem/iceage/
Learn more about the ice ages, including how alligators could live in the Arctic!

www.dkfindout.com/uk/history/stone-age/ice-age/
Discover how Neanderthals lived during the Ice Age.

GLOSSARY

carnivore animal that eats only meat

climate usual weather in a place

extinct no longer living; an extinct animal is one that has no more of its kind

glacial describes a period during which glaciers expand due to cooling temperatures

herbivore animal that eats only plants

hypothermia life-threatening condition that occurs when a person's body temperature falls several degrees below normal

megafauna large animals that lived around the time of the Ice Age

omnivore animal that eats both plants and other animals

predator animal that hunts other animals for food

prey animal hunted by another animal

tundra cold area where the soil under the ground is permanently frozen

BIBLIOGRAPHY

Carr, Ada, "We're Due For Another Ice Age But Climate Change May Push It Back Another 100,000 Years, Researchers Say," The Weather Channel, weather.com/news/climate/news/ice-age-climate-change-earth-glacial-interglacial-period, Accessed June 24, 2019.

"Global Climate Change: Evidence and Causes," Down to Earth Climate Change globalclimate.ucr.edu/resources.html, Accessed 24 June 2019.

Marshall, Michael, "The History of Ice on Earth," May 24, 2010, New Scientist, www.newscientist.com/article/dn18949-the-history-of-ice-on-earth/, Accessed 24 June 2019.

Salleh, Anna, "Ice Age Australians Sheltered in Caves," News in Science, September 24, 2007, www.abc.net.au/science/news/stories/2007/2039661.htm, Accessed 24 June 2019.

"The Big Five Mass Extinctions," COSMOS: The Science of Everything, cosmosmagazine.com/palaeontology/big-five-extinctions, Accessed 24 June 2019.

University of St. Andrews, "The Last Ice Age," July 3, 2014, phys.org/news/2014-07-ice-age.html, Accessed 24 June 2019.

"When Have Ice Ages Occurred?" Illinois State Museum, iceage.museum.state.il.us/content/when-have-ice-ages-occurred, Accessed 24 June 2019.

INDEX